HOW TO SOLVE TIME VALUE OF MONEY PROBLEMS WITH THE BAIIPLUS™ CALCULATOR

William F. Rentz, Ph.D., LIFA

and

Alfred L. Kahl, Ph.D., LIFA

Dedication

To my grandchildren
Abbey, Kaelen, and Andrew
W.F.R.

To Lola
A.L.K.

ABOUT THE AUTHORS

William F. Rentz

Dr. Rentz is a professor of finance at the Telfer School of Management of the University of Ottawa. He has served on the University of Ottawa Pension Plan Committee for many years. During his time on the committee, this pension plan increased its assets under management from $200 million to over $1.5 Billion now and is among the top 100 pension funds in Canada.

Dr. Rentz earned his S.B. from the Massachusetts Institute of Technology (MIT) and his A.M. and Ph.D. from the University of Rochester. He is a Licensed International Financial Analyst (LIFA).

Dr. Rentz is the author of many textbooks and academic journal articles. He is also co-author of ***Financial Mathematics with MS Excel: Time Value of Money*** which is available from: https://www.createspace.com/4975867

Alfred L. Kahl

Dr. Kahl is a professor of finance (retired) at the Telfer School of Management of the University of Ottawa. He was Associate Dean, Graduate Programs and Director of the MBA Program. He also served on the University of Ottawa Pension Plan Committee for 13 years. He has been teaching online MBA courses since 2001 for Baker College Online.

Dr. Kahl earned his B.A. from the University of Maryland, his M.B.A. from the University of Pittsburgh, and his Ph.D. from the University of Florida. He is a Licensed International Financial Analyst (LIFA).

Dr. Kahl is the author of many textbooks and academic journal articles. He is also co-author of *Financial Mathematics with MS Excel: Time Value of Money* which is available from: https://www.createspace.com/4975867

PREFACE

Because you could invest money today to earn a return, the value of a dollar today is not the same as the value of a dollar tomorrow. Thus, the principle of time value equivalence allows us to compare monetary values from different time periods. One of the most important uses of time value equivalence is investment decision making. Business managers forecast cash flows from potential investment projects and then discount them to present value to compare that present value with the cost of making the investment. If the net present value is positive, they then make the investment. Individual decision makers use the same procedure when deciding whether or not to buy a common stock.

This book is a brief guide for the use of the Texas Instruments BAIIPLUS™ financial calculator to solve time value of money problems that are of the most interest to financial managers and investors by using the built-in Time Value of Money, Cash Flow, Amortization, and Interest Conversion Worksheets.

This book presents detailed step-by-step instructions for solving the most important time value of money problems with the BAIIPLUS™ calculator along with brief explanations of the relevant financial theory related to the selected problems that are discussed herein. Thus, it provides not only the "**how to**" but also the "**why**" of time value of money.

TABLE OF CONTENTS

CHAPTER 1

ESSENTIAL CALCULATOR OPERATIONS

Introduction

The Texas Instruments BAIIPLUS™ calculator is an inexpensive tool for efficiently solving complex time value of money (TVM) financial problems.

This calculator is one of the permitted calculators for the Chartered Financial Analyst (CFA), Licensed International Financial Analyst (LIFA), Certified Financial Planner (CFP), and Financial Risk Manager (FRM) professional designation exams.

This book explains how to use the built-in worksheets of the BAIIPLUS™ calculator to solve time value of money problems.

In particular, this book illustrates the use of the Time Value of Money, Cash Flow, Amortization, and Interest Conversion worksheets that are of most interest to financial managers and investors.

This first chapter discusses the most important calculator operations.

Turning the Calculator On and Off

In this book, the calculator keys of the BAIIPLUS™ are enclosed in brackets.

The [ON/OFF] key is on the upper right corner of the keyboard. The [ON/OFF] key is a toggle switch. Press it once and the calculator turns on. Press it again and the calculator turns off. If you forget to turn off the calculator, it will automatically turn off about ten minutes after your last keystroke.

Turn on the calculator. Unless you have changed the factory default setting for the number of decimal places displayed, the display will show 0.00.

Press the [7][.][8][9][ENTER] keys and 7.89 will be displayed.

Turn the calculator off and then on again. Note that 0.00 will now be displayed. Turning the calculator off does **not** affect any data stored in the calculator, but it will erase any number showing on the screen.

Using the [2ND] key

Virtually every key on the BAIIPLUS™ has two functions. Each key's primary function is noted on the key itself, while the secondary function label of the key appears above the key.

To invoke the second function of a key, press the [2ND] key first. The [2ND] key is near the upper left corner of the calculator keyboard on the second row, and it is a distinctively different color from the other keys. The [2ND] key is also distinctive because there is no label above it.

Pressing the [2ND] key places a 2ND symbol in the upper left corner of the display. If the 2ND symbol appears, look only at the labels above the keys.

Press the [2ND] key again and the symbol disappears. The [2ND] key is a toggle key like the [ON/OFF] key.

Clearing Calculator Entries and Memories

The most commonly used methods of clearing data are:

KEYSTROKES	RESULT
[→]	Clears digits in the display, one at a time if you make a mistake entering data
[CE/C]	Clears the entire display, but **not** the memory
[2ND][CLR TVM]	Clears the TVM Worksheet if you are working within it
[2ND][CLR WORK]	Except for TVM, clears the current worksheet
[2ND][MEM][2ND] [CLR WORK]	Clears all memory locations and the display as well

Clearing the calculator is extremely important because unwanted data in memory can result in improper calculations, hence wrong answers.

It is best to get into the habit of automatically clearing memory before starting a calculation by using the appropriate keystrokes indicated above.

Occasionally, you may purposely want to save data, but usually you will be entering all new data. So, starting with a clear memory is the safest approach.

Changing Number of Decimal Places Displayed

To change the number of decimal places from 2 to 8, press [2ND][FORMAT][8][ENTER][CE/C] and 8.00000000 will be displayed.

To change from 8 places back to 2, press [2ND][FORMAT][2][ENTER][CE/C] and 2.00 will be displayed.

When doing financial calculations, it is customary to set the display to 2 decimal places. This is convenient when working with dollars and cents.

However, if more precision is desired, it is often better to use 6 or even 8 decimal places when dealing with interest rates and rates of return. (The minimum number of decimal places displayed is 0 and the maximum is 9).

Changing Number of Payments per Year (P/Y)

An important setting that can cause problems is the payments per year setting. Press [2ND][P/Y] to check the current setting, and the display shows the setting for payments/year.

The calculator usually is pre-set at 12 payments per year. That is, it assumes calculations will be done on a monthly basis. However, **many financial calculations require annual instead of monthly payments.**

Press [2ND][P/Y][1][ENTER][CE/C] to change the setting to only 1 payment per year, and the calculator will be set to use 1 payment per year.

To confirm this setting, press [2ND][P/Y] and P/Y = 1.00 should be displayed. Then press [CE/C] to leave the P/Y worksheet.

Unless needed for other work, **it is customary to leave the calculator setting at 1 payment per year.**

Press [2ND][P/Y][1][2][ENTER][CE/C] to restore the calculator to 12 payments per year, and the calculator will be reset to 12 payments per year.

Of course, you can set the number of payments per year to whatever is required. For example, you could press [2ND][P/Y][2][ENTER][CE/C] if 2 payments per year were appropriate for your desired calculation.

Changing Compounding Frequency (C/Y)

Virtually all financial calculators assume that the number of payments per year is equal to the compounding frequency per year. One of the great features of the BAIIPLUS™ is that it permits the compounding frequency to be different from the number of payments per year.

Set the payments per year to 4 by pressing the [2ND][P/Y][4][ENTER] keys to obtain P/Y = 4.00.

When one changes the payments per year (P/Y), the compounding frequency per year (C/Y) is automatically set to the same value. To see this, press the down arrow key and C/Y = 4.00 is displayed.

Suppose, however, that you want the compounding per year to be 12. Press [1][2][ENTER] and C/Y = 12.00 is displayed.

When one changes the compounding per year (C/Y), the number of payments per year (P/Y) remains at its previous value. To check that P/Y has **not** changed, press the down arrow key and P/Y = 4.00 is displayed.

We recommend that you now press [1][ENTER] to restore both P/Y and C/Y to 1.00 and press [CE/C] to exit.

Changing END Mode to BGN Mode to END Mode

The BAIIPLUS™ factory default setting for the mode toggle switch is the END mode.

This is appropriate for a stream of even payments called an **ordinary** or **regular annuity**, where each payment occurs at the **end** of the period.

Press [2ND][BGN][2ND][SET][CE/C] to analyze an **annuity due,** where a series of level payments occur at the **beginning** of each period, The BGN symbol appears in the upper right hand corner of the display. Now the BAIIPLUS™ analyzes the cash flows based on beginning of period payments.

To restore the calculator to the END mode, simply repeat the keystrokes [2ND][BGN][2ND][SET][CE/C]. Now the BGN symbol disappears from the upper right hand corner of the display.

Thus, the keystrokes [2ND][BGN][2ND][SET][CE/C] comprise a toggle that switches between calculator annuity modes.

CHAPTER 2

TVM CALCULATIONS: LUMP SUMS

Introduction

The most basic principle of the time value of money (TVM) is that a dollar today is worth more than a dollar in one year or at any future time. If one has a dollar today, one can invest that dollar to earn more than a dollar to be received in one year. The essence of time value of money (TVM) calculations is to determine a **time value equivalence** given an interest rate.

For example, if one could earn 10% in one year, then a dollar today is time value equivalent to $1 x 1.10 = $1.10 one year from now. If 10% is also the prevailing interest rate in the second year and interest is compounded annually, then $1 today is also time value equivalent to $1.00 x 1.10^2 = $1.21 in two years. The dollar today is referred to as a present value (PV). The $1.10 would be the time value equivalent future value (FV) in one year. The $1.21 would be the time value equivalent FV in two years.

This chapter discusses the Time Value of Money Worksheet using only lump sums. The next chapter will introduce even periodic cash flows into TVM calculations.

To simplify the discussions, taxes are ignored in all of the examples used throughout this book.

Time Value of Money (TVM) Variables

The five TVM variables for basic financial calculations are the number of periods (N), the interest rate (I/Y), the present value (PV), the periodic payments (PMT), and the future value (FV). The TVM keys are the only keys on the third row of the calculator in the order shown:

[N]   [I/Y]   [PV]   [PMT]   [FV]

In general, TVM problems involve these five variables. Usually four are known and the fifth is unknown.

Lump Sums Using Time Value of Money Worksheet

First, let us consider TVM calculations with single (lump) sums. In this situation, there are no periodic payments, *viz.* PMT = 0.

Thus, be sure to either press [2ND][CLR TVM] before entering any data, which sets PMT = 0, or enter 0 as the PMT when entering the input data.

Example 1: FV (Lump Sum Loan Repayment)

What is the future value (FV) of $7,091.90 at the end of 4 years, if the interest rate is compounded annually at 5%? That is, if you borrowed $7,091.90 today at an annual compound interest rate of 5%, how much money would you have to repay in four years?

First, press the [2ND][P/Y][1][ENTER][CE/C] keys to set the payments per year to 1.

Second, press the [2ND][CLR TVM] keys to clear the TVM memory registers.

Third, enter the following data:

KEYSTROKES	DISPLAY
[4][N]	N = 4.00
[5][I/Y]	I/Y – 5.00
[7][0][9][1][.][9][0][PV]	PV = 7,091.90

Finally, press [CPT][FV] to compute FV = -8,620.25.

Thus, $7,091.90 is time value equivalent to $8,620.25 in 4 years when the interest rate is 5% compounded annually.

The BAIIPLUS™ is programmed so that if the PV of a lump sum is displayed as a plus, then the FV is displayed as minus and vice versa. This is because the calculator assumes that one is an inflow and the other is an outflow (i.e. a **negative** inflow).

Example 2: PV (What Can You Borrow Today?)

How much can you borrow today if a lump sum repayment of $8,620.25 is due in four years and the interest rate is five percent compounded annually?

First, press the [2ND][P/Y][1][ENTER][CE/C] keys to set the payments per year to 1.

Second, press the [2ND][CLR TVM] keys to clear the TVM memory registers.

Third, enter the following data:

KEYSTROKES	DISPLAY
[4][N]	N = 4.00
[5][I/Y]	I/Y = 5.00
[8][6][2][0][.][2][5][+/-][FV]	FV = -8,620.25

Finally, to compute PV = 7,091.90 press the [CPT][PV] keys.

In other words, a PV today of $7,091.90 is time value equivalent to $8,620.25 in 4 years at an annual compound interest rate of 5%. This time value equivalence, of course, is consistent with the result of Example 1.

Note that it is extremely important that one uses the [+/-] key to change the sign to indicate that the FV of $8,620.25 is a cash outflow.

If you incorrectly use the keystroke sequence [-][8][6][2][0][.][2][5][FV], the calculator ignores the [-] keystroke and displays FV = 8,620.25. In this case, pressing the [CPT][PV] keys displays PV = -7,091.90.

The process of finding a present value is referred to as **discounting**. In this case the relevant periodic interest rate is often called the **discount rate**.

Example 3: Rate of Return or Growth Rate

Assume an asset can be purchased today for $7,091.90. It will return a lump sum payment of $8,620.25 at the end of 4 years. What rate of return would you earn if you bought the asset?

First, press the [2ND][P/Y][1][ENTER][CE/C] keys to set the payments per year to 1.

Second, press the [2ND][CLR TVM] keys to clear the TVM memory registers.

Third, enter the following data:

KEYSTROKES	DISPLAY
[4][N]	N = 4.00
[7][0][9][1][.][9][0][+/-][PV]	PV = -7,091.90
[8][6][2][0][.][2][5][FV]	FV = 8,620.25

Finally, press the [CPT][I/Y] keys to compute the rate of return and I/Y = 5.00 will be displayed. Thus, the BAIIPLUS™ calculated the rate of return to be 5.00%.

This rate of return calculation is consistent with the time value equivalents determined in Examples 1 and 2 and is called an **internal rate of return** (IRR). So long as the cash flows of a problem conform to the structure of the TVM Worksheet (i.e. a PV, level periodic payments, and an FV with a least two of these variables being non-zero with opposite signs), the [I/Y] function key can be used to calculate the IRR.

Later in this book, we will use the Cash Flow Worksheet to calculate the IRR of a more complex problem where periodic payments are **not** level.

In this example, -7,091.90 represents the money invested (i.e. an outflow) to buy the asset, and the 8,620.25 represents the money returned (i.e. an inflow) when the asset matures. **Entering the PV and FV with opposite signs is consistent with the sign convention discussed in Examples 1 and 2 above.**

If you enter both values as **positive** numbers, you will receive the **Error 5** message when you press the [CPT][I/Y] keys. Furthermore, you must enter -7,091.90 as [7][0][9][1][.][9][0][+/-][PV].

If you try to enter it as [-][7][0][9][1][.][9][0][PV] you will find that PV = 7,091.90 will be displayed and you will get the error message!

Note that this rate of return can also be viewed as the **growth rate** of your asset value due to compounding. **Often investors wish to know the growth rate of the dividends of a share of stock over time**.

The [I/Y] function key can be used to find this compound dividend growth rate so long as you remember to enter the starting dividend with the opposite sign of the ending dividend to avoid the Error 5 message.

Now suppose you learn that the asset will actually cost $7,146.19 instead of $7,091.90. What rate of return will you earn?

Enter [7][1][4][6][.][1][9][+/-][PV] to change the PV.

Then press [CPT][I/Y] to get 4.80%.

If you pay **more** for the asset, you earn a **lower** rate of return on it. The important thing, though, is that you can do "what if" analyses with the calculator.

Now do nothing except press [ON/OFF] to turn off the calculator.

Then turn on the calculator by pressing the [ON/OFF] key. The display shows 0.00. Is the memory erased? **Not** completely. What was on the screen is gone, but press [RCL][I/Y] to get I/Y = 4.80.

Example 4: Number (N) of Periods to Reach a Goal (Home Purchase)

Suppose you have inherited $30,000 from your late Uncle Jack, but you will need $36,500 to make a down payment on your dream home. If you can invest this lump sum of $30,000 at 4% compounded annually, how long will it take to reach your financial goal?

First, press the [2ND][P/Y][1][ENTER][CE/C] keys to set the payments per year to 1.

Second, press the [2ND][CLR TVM] keys to clear the TVM memory registers.

Third, enter the following data:

KEYSTROKES	DISPLAY
[4][I/Y]	I/Y = 4.00
[3][0][0][0][0][+/-][PV]	PV = -30,000.00
[3][6][5][0][0][FV]	FV = 36,500.00

Finally, press the [CPT][N] keys to compute N = 5.00. This is the number of periods required to achieve your financial goal.

Let us consider another example of savings for a financial goal.

Example 5: Number (N) of Periods to Reach a Goal (Retire)

Suppose you feel that you will need at least $1,000,000 in savings to adequately fund your retirement. You currently have $30,000 in savings, and you are 21 years old. If you can invest this lump sum at 8% compounded annually, at what age can you afford to retire?

First, press [2ND][P/Y][1][ENTER][CE/C] to set the payments per year to 1.

Second, press the [2ND][CLR TVM] keys to clear the TVM memory registers.

Third, enter the following data:

KEYSTROKES	DISPLAY
[8][I/Y]	I/Y = 8.00
[3][0][0][0][0][+/-][PV]	PV = -30,000.00
[1][0][0][0][0][0][0][FV]	FV = 1,000,000.00

Finally, press the [CPT][N] keys to compute N = 45.56.

So, if you can set aside $30,000 at age 21, you can retire at age 21 + 45.56, which is approximately age 67!

In the current very low interest rate environment, an 8% return is **not** achievable by investing in relatively low risk securities such as government bonds.

A more reasonable rate to assume is 4%. Setting I/Y = 4.00 and recalculating N yields N = 89.41 years or approximately at age 21 + 89 = 110.

Given current life expectancies, it appears that your financial plan is **not** feasible in your lifetime!

This suggests that you must plan to make periodic deposits to your savings account throughout your working career rather than a single lump sum deposit today.

The next chapter discusses level periodic payments.

CHAPTER 3

TVM CALCULATIONS: EVEN CASH FLOWS

Introduction

This chapter discusses time value of money (TVM) calculations with even cash flows of ordinary annuities and annuities due.

An **ordinary** or **regular annuity** is a series of even cash flows at the **end** of each period for a specified number of periods. Auto loans and home mortgages are the major loans by dollar amount for most consumers and are examples of ordinary annuities.

An **annuity due** is a series of level periodic payments at the **beginning** of each period for a specified number of periods. Lease payments for automobiles and apartments as well insurance premiums are examples of annuities due.

Even Periodic Cash Flows Using the TVM Worksheet

Annuity cash flows occur regularly over time, either at the end of each period or at the beginning of each period. Annuity problems can be solved by using The Time Value of Money Worksheet.

Timelines are often used to visualize TVM problems. Example 6 below illustrates the use of a timeline.

Example 6: FV of an Ordinary Annuity (Accumulated Savings)

Suppose that you wish to deposit $2,000 at the **end** of each year for 4 years. What is the FV of this annuity if the interest rate is 5 percent compounded annually? That is, how much money have you accumulated in your savings account at the end of 4 years?

The timeline below represents an ordinary annuity for 4 years of $2,000 per year using an annual interest rate of 5%.

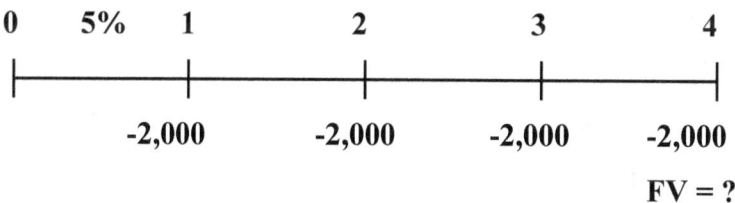

The four deposits of $2,000 must be entered into the calculator as negative numbers because these cash flows are considered to be outflows. Each deposit will earn 5% annual interest until the end of the four year period of time.

Make sure that the calculator is in the END mode by verifying that the BGN symbol does **not** appear in the upper right hand corner of the display.

If BGN appears in the display, press the toggle switch keystroke sequence [2ND][BGN][2ND][SET][CE/C] to restore the calculator to the END mode.

First, set the payments per year to 1 by pressing [2ND][P/Y][1][ENTER][CE/C].

Second, clear the TVM memory registers by pressing [2ND][CLR TVM].

Third, enter the following data:

KEYSTROKES	DISPLAY
[4][N]	N = 4.00
[5][I/Y]	I/Y = 5.00
[2][0][0][0][+/-][PMT]	PMT = -2,000.00

Finally, press [CPT][FV] to compute FV = 8,620.25

The ordinary annuity of $2,000 per year for 4 years is time value equivalent at a 5% annual interest rate to a lump sum FV of $8,620.25 at the end of 4 years. Note that this is the FV computed in Example 1 of the previous chapter. This means that this ordinary annuity is also time value equivalent to the PV of $7,091.90 originally borrowed in Example 1.

Example 7: FV of an Annuity Due (Accumulated Savings)

Redo Example 6 above as an annuity due. Recall that each payment of an **annuity due** occurs at the **beginning** of the period instead of at the **end** as with an **ordinary** or **regular annuity**. In essence, each payment occurs one period sooner.

The timeline below represents an annuity due of $2,000 per year for 4 years using an annual interest rate of 5%.

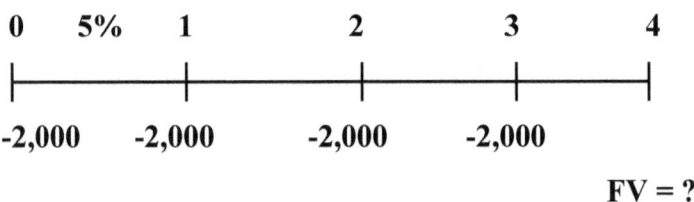

Check to see if the calculator is in the BGN mode by verifying that the BGN symbol appears in the upper right hand corner of the display. If BGN does **not** appear in the display, press the toggle switch keystroke sequence [2ND][BGN][2ND][SET][CE/C] to set the calculator to the BGN mode.

If you still have the Example 6 data entered, press the [CPT][FV] keys to compute FV = 9,051.26.

If you do **not** have the Example 6 data entered, first, with the calculator in the BGN mode, set the payments per year P/Y = 1 by pressing [2ND][P/Y][1][ENTER][CE/C].

Second, clear the TVM memory registers by pressing [2ND][CLR TVM].

Third, enter the following data:

KEYSTROKES	DISPLAY
[4][N]	N = 4.00
[5][I/Y]	I/Y = 5.00
[2][0][0][0][+/-][PMT]	PMT = -2,000.00

Finally, press [CPT][FV] to compute FV = 9,051.26.

Note that the FV of the annuity due is larger than the FV = 8,620.25 for the ordinary annuity.

This is because **each** payment of the annuity due is earning interest for 1 additional period.

Thus, the FV of the annuity due equals the FV of the ordinary annuity **times** (1 + periodic interest rate), *viz.*, $9,051.26 = $8,620.25 x (1 + 0.05).

Unless you are doing a series of annuity due calculations, we strongly recommend that you always return the calculator to the END mode after doing an annuity due calculation!

Change back to END mode by pressing [2ND][BGN][2ND][SET][CE/C]. In other words, the keystroke sequence [2ND][BGN][2ND][SET][CE/C] is a toggle switch that switches from the END mode to the BGN mode and vice versa.

Example 8: PV of an Ordinary Annuity (Borrowing)

What is the PV of the ordinary annuity in Example 6 above? That is, how much can you borrow today if you can repay $2,000 at the **end** of each year for 4 years when the compound annual interest rate is 5%?

The timeline below represents an ordinary annuity of $2,000 per year for 4 years using an annual interest rate of 5%.

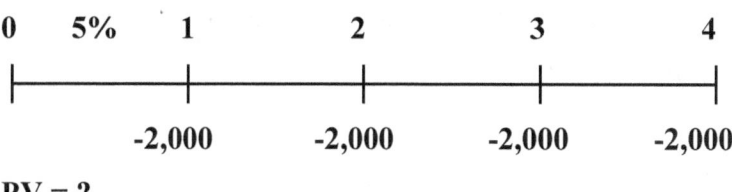

PV = ?

Make sure that you have returned the calculator to the END mode as discussed at the conclusion of Example 7. The calculator will be in the END mode if the BGN symbol does **not** appear in the upper right hand corner of the display.

If you have **not** yet returned the calculator to the END mode (i.e. the BGN symbol still appears in the display), press the toggle switch keystroke sequence [2ND][BGN][2ND][SET][CE/C].

If the data from Example 7 data is still entered in the calculator, enter 0 as the FV to override the 9,051.26. Then press [CPT][PV] to get PV = 7,091.90.

If the data from Example 7 is **not** in the calculator, first set P/Y = 1 by pressing [2ND][P/Y][1][ENTER][CE/C].

Second, clear the TVM memory registers by pressing [2ND][CLR TVM].

Third, enter the following data:

KEYSTROKES	DISPLAY
[4][N]	N = 4.00
[5][I/Y]	I/Y = 5.00
[2][0][0][0][+/-][PMT]	PMT = -2,000.00

Finally, press [CPT][PV] to compute PV = 7,091.90.

Note that the PV of this ordinary annuity is smaller than the FV of this ordinary annuity of 8,620.25 calculated in Example 6. **This is always true for any annuity evaluated with a positive interest rate.**

In this example, when interest is compounded at 5% annually, we have shown that the ordinary annual annuity of $2,000 for 4 years is time value equivalent to a PV of 7,091.90.

In Example 6, we showed that this same annuity is time value equivalent to an FV = 8,620.25 at the end of year 4. Thus, a PV = 7,091.90 must be time value equivalent to an FV = 8,620.25 at the end of year 4 when interest is compounded annually at 5%. Recall that we had already shown this time value equivalence in Examples 1 and 2 of the previous chapter.

Example 9: PV of an Annuity Due (Leasing)

Redo Example 8 above as an annuity due instead of a regular annuity.

The timeline below represents an annuity due of $2,000 per year for 4 years using an annual interest rate of 5%.

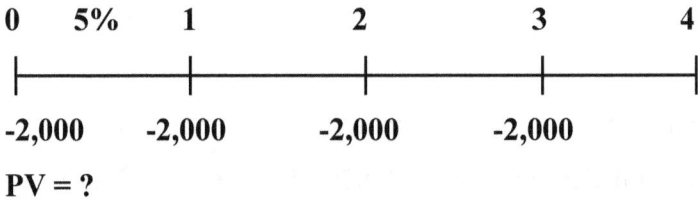

Check to see if your calculator is BGN mode by verifying that BGN appears in the upper right hand corner of the display. If BGN does **not** appear in the display, change to the BGN mode by pressing the toggle switch keystroke sequence [2ND][BGN][2ND][SET][CE/C]. The BGN symbol should now be displayed.

If you currently have the Example 8 data in your calculator, press [CPT][PV] keys to obtain PV = 7,446.50.

If you do **not** have the data from Example 8 in your calculator, first set the P/Y = 1 by pressing [2ND][P/Y][1][ENTER][CE/C].

Second, clear the TVM memory registers by pressing [2ND][CLR TVM].

Third, enter the following data as in Example 8:

KEYSTROKES	DISPLAY
[4][N]	N = 4.00
[5][I/Y]	I/Y = 5.00
[2][0][0][0][+/-][PMT]	PMT = -2,000.00

Finally, press [CPT][PV] to compute PV = 7,446.50.

Note that 7,091.90 x 1.05 = 7,446.50, where 7,091.90 is the PV of the ordinary annuity found in Example 8.

Whether you are calculating the PV or the FV of an annuity due, the annuity due value is always (1 + periodic interest rate) times the corresponding value for the ordinary annuity.

In other words, when computing the FV of an annuity due in comparison to an ordinary annuity, **every annuity due payment earns interest for 1 more period**.

Similarly, when computing the PV of an annuity due in comparison to an ordinary annuity, **every annuity due payment gets discounted for 1 less period**. The effect is the same.

For any positive interest rate, the value of the ordinary annuity understates the value of the corresponding annuity due by the factor (1 + periodic interest rate).

Example 10: Rate of Return: Ordinary Annuity

Suppose that you are offered the opportunity to invest $3,000 at the **end** of each year for the next 3 years. You are promised a return of $10,000 at the **end** of three years. You require a rate of return of 10% for investment of this degree of risk. Should you make this investment?

The timeline below represents an ordinary annuity for 3 years of $3,000 per year using an annual interest rate of ?%.

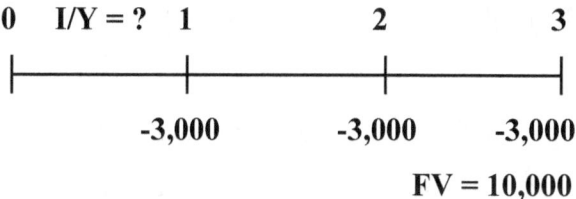

Make sure that the calculator is in the END mode by verifying that the BGN symbol does **not** appear in the upper right hand corner of the display. If the calculator is in the BGN mode, press the toggle switch keystroke sequence [2ND][BGN][2ND][SET][CE/C] to restore the calculator to the END mode.

First, set P/Y = 1 by pressing
[2ND][P/Y][1][ENTER][CE/C].

Second, clear the TVM memory registers by pressing
[2ND][CLR TVM].

Third, enter the following data:

KEYSTROKES	DISPLAY
[3][N]	N = 3.00
[3][0][0][0][+/-][PMT]	PMT = -3,000.00
[1][0][0][0][0][FV]	FV = 10,000.00

Finally, press the [CPT][I/Y] keys to compute I/Y = 10.73.
Thus, the investment earns an internal rate of return (IRR)
of 10.73%, which is greater than your required rate of
return of 10%. Hence, you should make the investment.

Example 11: Rate of Return: Annuity Due

Recalculate the rate of return for Example 10 when the payments are at the **beginning** of the period. Recall that you now are offered the opportunity to invest $3,000 at the **beginning** of each year for the next 3 years. You require a rate of return of 10% for investment of this degree of risk. Should you make this investment now if your required rate of return is still 10%?

The timeline below represents an annuity due of $3,000 per year for 3 years using an annual interest rate of ?%.

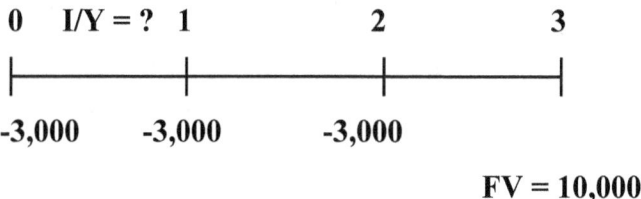

Make sure that the calculator is in the BGN mode by verifying that the BGN symbol appears in the upper right hand corner of the display. If the BGN symbol does **not** appear, press the toggle switch keystroke sequence [2ND][BGN][2ND][SET][CE/C] to set the calculator to the BGN mode.

If the data from Example 10 is still entered, press the [CPT][I/Y] keys to obtain [I/Y] = 5.36%.

If you do **not** have the Example 10 data entered, first set P/Y = 1 by pressing [2ND][P/Y][1][ENTER][CE/C].

Second, clear the TVM memory registers by pressing [2ND][CLR TVM].

Third, enter the following data:

KEYSTROKES	DISPLAY
[3][N]	N = 3.00
[3][0][0][0][+/-][PMT]	PMT = -3,000.00
[1][0][0][0][0][FV]	FV = 10,000.00

Finally, press [CPT][I/Y] to compute I/Y = 5.36%.

Since your required rate of return is still 10%, you should **not** make this investment because the IRR is less than your required rate of return. The IRR is lower because you have to make each of the periodic payments 1 period earlier, and this makes the investment unattractive in this example.

Example 12: Yield to Maturity (YTM) for a Bond

Bonds typically have maturity values of $1,000. (The maturity value is sometimes referred to as the face value or par value.) Most bonds have a stated nominal annual coupon rate, but the interest payments are made semi-annually at half of the stated rate. Thus, these payments are a semi-annual ordinary annuity during the life of the bond.

Consider a bond that matures in 20 years (i.e. 40 semi-annual periods), has a stated coupon rate of 10%, and is selling for $900. What is the yield to maturity (YTM) for this bond?

For the typical bond, the YTM is a nominal annual interest rate based on semi-annual compounding just like the stated coupon interest rate. The timeline is shown below:

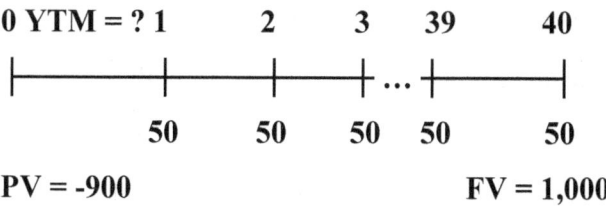

Make sure that the calculator is in the END mode by verifying that the BGN symbol does **not** appear in the upper right hand corner of the display.

If the calculator is in the BGN mode, return it to the END mode by pressing the toggle switch keystroke sequence [2ND][BGN][2ND][SET][CE/C].

First, set P/Y = 2 by pressing [2ND][P/Y][2][ENTER][CE/C].

Second, clear the TVM memory registers by pressing [2ND][CLR TVM].

Third, enter the following data, noting that the semi-annual interest payments will be ½ x 10% x $1,000 = $50:

KEYSTROKES	DISPLAY
[2][0][2ND][xP/Y][N]	N = 40.00
[9][0][0][+/-][PV]	PV = -900.00
[5][0][PMT]	PMT = 50.00
[1][0][0][0][FV]	FV = 1,000.00

Finally, press [CPT][I/Y] to compute I/Y = 11.27. Thus, the YTM for this bond is 11.27%. This should be compared to your required rate of return to determine if this is an attractive investment. So, if you require an YTM of 11% for investments of this degree of risk, then this bond is an attractive investment because it exceeds your required rate of return.

Note that the YTM was **more** than the stated coupon interest rate. **Whenever the selling price of the bond is less than the maturity value, the YTM will be more than the coupon interest rate and vice versa.**

The next example demonstrates that if the YTM is **less** than the coupon rate, the bond will sell for **more** than its maturity value.

Example 13: Price (PV) of a Bond

Consider a bond that matures in 20 years and has a stated coupon rate of 10%. For a bond of this degree or riskiness, you require a yield to maturity (YTM) of 9%. What is the maximum price that you would be willing to pay to buy this bond?

The timeline below represents an ordinary annuity of $50 per 40 periods using a nominal annual interest rate of 9%.

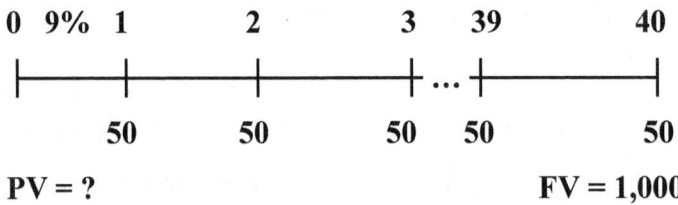

Make sure that the calculator is in the END mode by verifying that the BGN symbol does **not** appear in the display. If BGN does appear, press the toggle switch keystroke sequence [2ND][BGN][2ND][SET][CE/C] to restore the calculator to the END mode.

If you currently have the Example 12 data in your calculator, press [9][I/Y] to enter your required YTM and then press [CPT][PV] to compute PV = -1,092.01.

If you do **not** have the data from Example 12 in your calculator, first set P/Y = 2 by pressing [2ND][P/Y][2][ENTER][CE/C].

Second, clear the TVM memory registers by pressing [2ND][CLR TVM].

Third, enter the following data, noting that the semi-annual interest payments will be ½ x 10% x $1,000 = $50:

KEYSTROKES	DISPLAY
[2][0][2ND][x P/Y][N]	N = 40.00
[9][I/Y]	I/Y = 9.00
[5][0][PMT]	PMT = 50.00
[1][0][0][0][FV]	FV = 1,000.00

Finally, press [CPT][PV] to compute PV = -1,092.01. Thus, the maximum price that you would be willing to pay for this bond is $1,092.01 in order for you to earn at least your required YTM of 9%.

Note that your required YTM was **less** than the stated coupon interest rate. **Whenever the required YTM is less than the coupon interest rate, the maximum price that you will be willing to pay will be more than the maturity value and vice versa.**

Example 14: Number (N) of Ordinary Annuity PMTs for a Goal (Retire)

In Example 5 of the previous chapter, a rather large lump sum payment of $30,000 for someone only 21 years old was insufficient to achieve a retirement goal of $1,000,000 when the interest rate was 4% compounded annually. In that example, we suggested that a feasible strategy would require periodic payments throughout a person's working career.

Suppose you are still 21 years old and feel that you will need at least $1,000,000 in savings to adequately fund your retirement. You plan to deposit $5,000 at the **end** of every year until you retire. If you can invest these periodic payments at 4% compounded annually, how long will it take to reach your financial goal of FV = $1,000,000 at retirement?

The timeline below represents an ordinary annuity of $5,000 per year for N years using an annual interest rate of 4%.

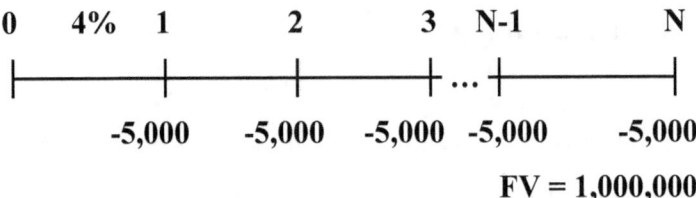

Check to see that the calculator is in the END mode by verifying that the BGN symbol does **not** appear in the display. If BGN does appear, press the toggle switch keystroke sequence [2ND][BGN][2ND][SET][CE/C] to restore the calculator to the END mode.

First, set P/Y = 1.00 by pressing [2ND][P/Y][1][ENTER][CE/C].

Second, clear the TVM memory registers by pressing [2ND][CLR TVM].

Third, enter the following data:

KEYSTROKES	DISPLAY
[4][I/Y]	I/Y = 4.00
[5][0][0][0][+/-][PMT]	PMT = -5,000.00
[1][0][0][0][0][0][0][FV]	FV = 1,000,000.00

Finally, press [CPT][N] to compute N = 56.02. Thus, the number of periods required to achieve your financial goal is 56.02 years.

So, if you can save $5,000 at the end of each year starting at age 21, you can retire at age 77!

Example 15: Number (N) of Annuity Due PMTs to Reach a Goal (Retire)

Redo Example 14 with annuity due payments. How much sooner can you retire?

The timeline below represents an annuity due of $5,000 per year for N years using an annual interest rate of 4%.

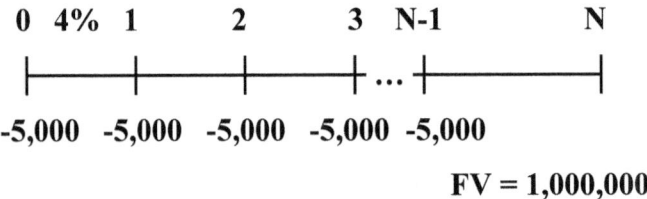

Check to see that the calculator is in the BGN mode by verifying that the BGN symbol appears in the display. If BGN does **not** appear, press the toggle switch keystroke sequence [2ND][BGN][2ND][SET][CE/C] to set the calculator to the BGN mode.

If you still have the Example 14 data entered, press the [CPT][N] keys to compute N = 55.14.

If you do **not** have the data entered from the previous example, first set P/Y = 1.00 by pressing [2ND][P/Y][1][ENTER][CE/C].

Second, clear the TVM memory registers by pressing [2ND][CLR TVM].

Third, enter the following data:

KEYSTROKES	DISPLAY
[4][I/Y]	I/Y = 4.00
[5][0][0][0][+/-][PMT]	PMT = -5,000.00
[1][0][0][0][0][0][0][FV]	FV = 1,000,000.00

Finally, press [CPT][N] to compute N = 55.14. Thus, the number of periods required to achieve your financial goal is 55.14 years.

So, if you can save $5,000 at the **beginning** of each year starting at age 21, you can retire at age 76 or approximately one year earlier than saving at the **end** of each year!

Example 16: Ordinary Annuity Payments to Reach a Goal (Retire)

In the previous two examples, we determined that you would be 77 (76) before you could retire when you made periodic savings deposits at the end (beginning) of the year.

Now suppose that you are willing to increase the size of the periodic payments at the **end** of each year so that you can retire at age 67, which is 46 years from today. If the interest rate is still 4% compounded annually and you still wish to achieve a FV = $1,000,000, how much must you deposit in your savings account at the **end** of each year for the next 46 years?

The timeline below represents an ordinary annuity of $? per year for 46 years using an annual interest rate of 4%.

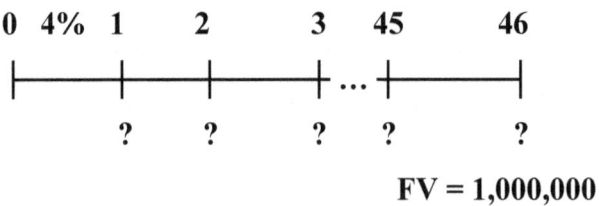

Make sure that the calculator is in the END mode by verifying that the BGN symbol does **not** appear in the upper right hand corner of the display. If BGN does appear, change to the END mode by pressing the toggle switch keystroke sequence [2ND][BGN][2ND][SET][CE/C].

First, set P/Y = 1.00 by pressing [2ND][P/Y][1][ENTER][CE/C].

Second, clear the TVM memory registers by pressing [2ND][CLR TVM].

Third, enter the following data:

KEYSTROKES	DISPLAY
[4][6][N]	N = 46.00
[4][I/Y]	I/Y = 4.00
[1][0][0][0][0][0][0][FV]	FV = 1,000,000.00

Finally, press [CPT][PMT] to compute PMT = -7,882.05.

Thus, saving an additional $7,882.05 - $5,000 = $2,882.05 per year allows you to retire 77 – 67 = 10 years earlier.

Suppose you still wish to retire at age 67 but that you are age 30 now. Thus, you must reset N to N = 37.00.

Press [CPT][PMT] to compute PMT = -12,239.57.

Deferring your savings plan for nine years means that your annual deposits must increase by $12,239.57 - $7,521.89 = $4,717.68. Thus, it behooves you to start saving early for retirement!

Example 17: Annuity Due Payments to Reach a Goal (Retire)

Redo Example 16 with annuity due payments.

The timeline below represents an annuity due of $? per year for 46 years using an annual interest rate of 4%.

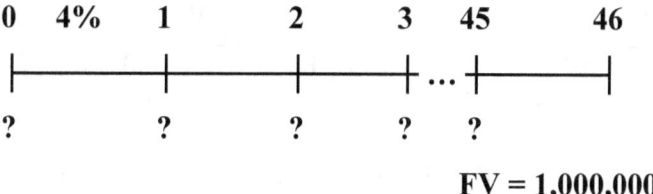

FV = 1,000,000

Check to see if the calculator is in the END mode by verifying that the BGN symbol does **not** appear in the upper right hand corner of the display.

If BGN does **not** appear, set the calculator to the BGN mode by pressing the toggle switch keystroke sequence [2ND][BGN][2ND][SET][CE/C] so that BGN now appears in the display.

First set P/Y = 1.00 by pressing [2ND][P/Y][1][ENTER][CE/C].

Second, clear the TVM memory registers by pressing [2ND][CLR TVM].

Third, enter the following data:

KEYSTROKES	DISPLAY
[4][6][N]	N = 46.00
[4][I/Y]	I/Y = 4.00
[1][0][0][0][0][0][0][FV]	FV = 1,000,000.00

Finally, press [CPT][PMT] to compute PMT = -7,578.89.

Note that **for any positive interest rate, the annuity due payment will be smaller than the ordinary annuity payment**. To be precise, each ordinary annuity payment must be the annuity due payment x (1 + periodic interest rate), *viz.*, $7,882.05 = $7,578.89 x 1.04.

Thus, once again we note that it behooves you to start saving early for retirement!

CHAPTER 4

LOAN AMORTIZATION & INTEREST CONVERSION

Introduction

A loan **amortization schedule** shows how much of each periodic loan payment is interest and how much is principal repayment. Because the periodic payment is comprised of both interest and principal, it is often referred to as a **blended payment**. The amortization schedule typically also shows the beginning and remaining balance of the principal outstanding. The BAIIPLUS™ Amortization Worksheet is useful in constructing an amortization schedule.

The **Interest Conversion Worksheet** can be used to convert annual nominal or annual percentage rates into effective periodic interest rates for solving problems that require multiple compounding periods.

These topics are discussed in this chapter.

Example 18: Interest & Principal of an Amortized Loan

Determine the interest and principal paid each year and the balance at the end of each year on a 4 year $10,000 amortizing loan that carries an interest rate of 10.5%. The payments are due at the end of each annual period.

The timeline below represents an ordinary annuity of $? per year for 4 years using an annual interest rate of 10.5%.

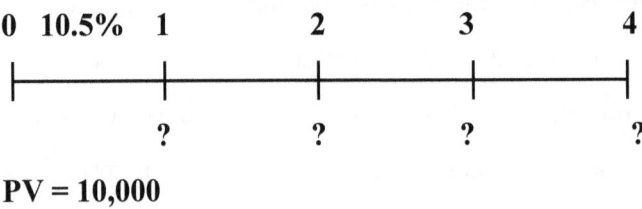

Make sure that the calculator is in the END mode by verifying that the BGN symbol does **not** appear in the display. If BGN does appear, restore the calculator to the END mode by pressing the toggle switch keystroke sequence [2ND][BGN][2ND][SET][CE/C].

First, set P/Y = 1.00 by pressing [2ND][P/Y][1][ENTER][CE/C].

Second, clear the TVM memory registers by pressing [2ND][CLR TVM].

Third, enter the following data:

KEYSTROKES	DISPLAY
[4][N]	N = 4.00
[1][0][.][5][I/Y]	I/Y = 10.50
[1][0][0][0][0][PV]	PV = 10,000.00

Finally, press [CPT][PMT] to compute PMT = -3,188.92.

This payment is a **blended payment** of interest and principal repayment.

Now we will use the Amortization Worksheet to generate an amortization schedule for this loan. The **relevant keystrokes** to start using the Amortization Worksheet are shown below:

KEYSTROKES	DISPLAY
[2ND][AMORT] [2ND][CLR WORK]	P1 = 1.00 (from period 1)
[↓]	P2 = 1.00 (show each PMT)
[↓]	BAL = 7,861.08
[↓]	PRN = -2,138.92
[↓]	INT = -1,050.00

To view the results for the second payment, begin by pressing [↓][CPT]. This displays P1 = 2.00. Pressing [↓] again displays P2 = 2.00. Use the [↓] key repeatedly to view the second period ending balance, principal payment, and interest payment. Repeat the above steps for the ensuing payments and fill in the following amortization schedule:

Amortization Schedule

Month	Beginning Balance	Interest Portion	Principal Portion	Remaining Balance
0				10,000.00
1	10,000.00	1,050.00	2,138.92	7,861.08
2	7,861.08	825.41	2,363.51	5,497.57
3	5,497.57	577.24	2,611.68	2,885.89
4	2,885.89	303.02	2,885.90	-0.01

Note that the ending balance is **negative** one cent. Thus, to exactly amortize this loan over four years, the last blended payment must be one cent **less**, which is $3,188.92 - .01 = $3,188.91. Thus, the last principal payment will also be one cent less, which is $2,885.90 - .01 = $2,885.89.

Note also that the interest and principal repayments are shown as **negative** numbers on the BAIIPLUS™ because they represent cash outflows.

Example 19: U.S. Mortgage: Monthly Payments

Suppose you are considering buying a new home in Florida. The bank quotes a nominal annual mortgage interest rate of 6% with monthly compounding and an amortization period of 30 years. Your dream home costs $300,000 and you have saved $60,000 for the down payment. Thus, you want to borrow $300,000 - $60,000 = $240,000. You want to make monthly payments because you are paid monthly. What is your monthly mortgage payment?

The timeline below represents an ordinary annuity of $? monthly for 30 years, which is 30 x 12 = 360 months, using a nominal annual interest rate of 6%?

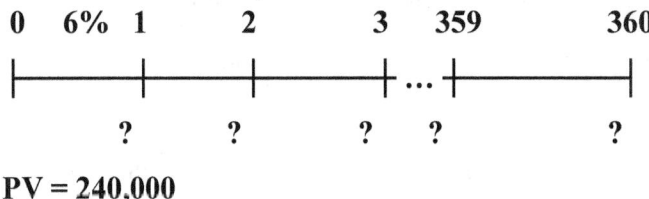

PV = 240,000

Make sure that your calculator is set to the END mode and that the BGN symbol does **not** appear in the display.

If BGN does appear, restore the calculator to the END mode by pressing the toggle switch keystroke sequence [2ND][BGN][2ND][SET][CE/C].

Since interest on U.S. mortgages is compounded monthly, you first need to set P/Y = 12.00 by pressing [2ND][P/Y][1][2][ENTER].

Second, clear the TVM memory registers by pressing [CE/C][2ND][CLR TVM].

Third, enter the following data:

KEYSTROKES	DISPLAY
[3][0][2ND][xP/Y][N]	N = 360.00
[6][I/Y]	I/Y = 6.00
[2][4][0][0][0][0][PV]	PV = 240,000.00

Finally, press [CPT][PMT] to compute PMT = -1,438.92. This payment is a blended payment of interest and principal repayment.

Now we can use the Amortization Worksheet to generate amortization information for the first and last month of the mortgage by entering the following data:

KEYSTROKES	DISPLAY
[2ND][AMORT] [2ND][CLR WORK]	P1 = 1.00 (start from period 1)
[↓]	P2 = 1.00 (show each payment)
[↓]	BAL = 239,761.08
[↓]	PRN = -238.92
[↓]	INT = -1,200.00
[↓][3][6][0][ENTER]	P1 = 360.00
[↓][3][6][0][ENTER]	P2 = 360.00
[↓]	BAL = 1.38
[↓]	PRN = -1,431.75
[↓]	INT = -7.17

Thus, we have the following amortization schedule:

Amortization Schedule

Month	Beginning Balance	Interest Portion	Principal Portion	Remaining Balance
0				240,000.00
1	240,000.00	1,200.00	238.92	239,761.08
360	1,433.13	7.17	1,431.75	1.38

Note that the ending balance is $1.38. Thus, to exactly amortize this loan over 30 years, the last blended monthly payment must be $1.38 more or $1,438.92 + $1.38 = $1,440.30. This means that the last principal payment will also be $1.38 more or $1,431.75 + $1.38 = $1,433.13.

Note also that the interest and principal repayments are shown as **negative** numbers on the BAIIPLUS™ because they represent cash outflows.

Since this mortgage is for the lengthy period of 30 years, note that the first month blended payment is mostly interest and little principal repayment; whereas, the last blended payment is virtually all principal repayment and little interest payment.

With each monthly blended payment, a portion goes to repayment of principal. This means that the succeeding month will require a smaller interest payment and consequently a larger principal repayment.

Example 20: U.S. Mortgage with Semi-Monthly Payments

Redo Example 19, except that you now want to make semi-monthly payments because you are paid semi-monthly. Recall that the bank quotes a nominal annual mortgage interest rate of 6% with monthly compounding and an amortization period of 30 years.

Your dream home costs $300,000 and you have saved $60,000 for the down payment. Thus, you want to borrow $300,000 - $60,000 = $240,000. What is your semi-monthly payment?

The timeline below represents an ordinary annuity of $? semi-monthly for 30 years; this is 30 x 24 = 720 periods, using a nominal annual interest rate of 6%.

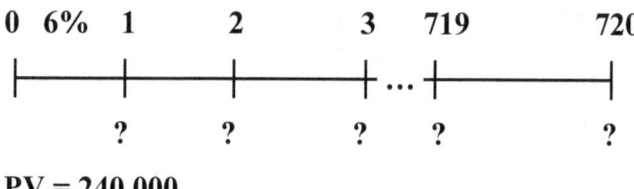

PV = 240,000

Make sure that your calculator is set to the END mode and that the BGN symbol does **not** appear in the display. If BGN does appear, restore the calculator to the END mode by pressing the toggle switch keystroke sequence [2ND][BGN][2ND][SET][CE/C].

Realize that interest on U.S. mortgages is still compounded monthly but that you are paying twice per month, which is 24 times per year or 30 x 24 = 720 times in 30 years.

First, press [2ND][P/Y][2][4][ENTER] to set P/Y = 24.00 and press [↓][1][2][ENTER] to set C/Y = 12.00.

Second, clear the TVM memory registers by pressing [CE/C][2ND][CLR TVM].

Third, enter the following data:

KEYSTROKES	DISPLAY
[3][0][2ND][xP/Y][N]	N = 720.00
[6][I/Y]	I/Y = 6.00
[2][4][0][0][0][0][PV]	PV = 240,000.00

Finally, press [CPT][PMT] to compute PMT = -718.56.

This payment is a blended payment of interest and principal repayment. (If you wish to construct a loan amortization schedule, follow the **relevant steps in Example 18)**.

Since you are making mortgage payments more frequently, you are repaying principal sooner. This means that the total interest charged over the life of the loan and also in any month will be **less** by making semi-monthly payments than making monthly payments. This also means that total blended payments over the life of the loan and also in any month will be less by making the more frequent semi-monthly payments. To see this, note that the semi-monthly blended payments for any month are 2 x $718.56 = $1,437.12 < $1,438.92, which is the blended monthly mortgage payment.

Thus, the more frequently one pays, the lower the total interest and total blended payments will be.

Nevertheless, the more frequent blended payments are just a different annuity stream that is also time value equivalent to the amount borrowed.

Example 21: Vehicle Loan with Bi-Weekly Payments

Suppose you are considering buying a new SUV. The dealer quotes a nominal annual interest rate of 3% with monthly compounding and an amortization period of 6 years. Your SUV costs $30,000 and you want to borrow the full $30,000.

You want to make bi-weekly payments because you are paid bi-weekly. What is your bi-weekly loan payment if you assume for simplicity that there are **exactly** 26 bi-weekly periods per year or 26 x 6 = 156 payments in 6 years?

The timeline below represents an ordinary annuity of $? for 156 periods using a nominal annual interest rate of 3%.

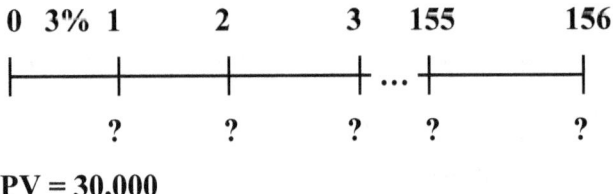

PV = 30,000

Make sure that your calculator is set to the END mode and the BGN symbol is **not** displayed.

If BGN does appear, restore the calculator to the END mode by pressing the toggle switch keystroke sequence [2ND][BGN][2ND][SET][CE/C].

First, press [2ND][P/Y][2][6][ENTER] to set P/Y = 26.00 and press [↓][1][2][ENTER] to set C/Y = 12.00.

Second, clear the TVM memory registers by pressing [CE/C][2ND][CLR TVM].

Third, enter the following data:

KEYSTROKES	DISPLAY
[6][2ND][xP/Y][N]	N = 156.00
[3][I/Y]	I/Y = 3.00
[3][0][0][0][0][PV]	PV = 30,000.00

Finally, press [CPT][PMT] to compute PMT = -210.23. This payment is a blended payment of interest and principal repayment. (If you wish to construct a loan amortization schedule, follow the **relevant steps in Example 18)**.

The BAIIPLUS™ is one of a very few financial calculators that permits users to set the compounding frequency different from the payment frequency. This allows users to avoid the heavy lifting of calculating an effective payment period rate through an Interest Conversion Worksheet.

If you are curious about what the effective bi-weekly payment period rate is for this vehicle loan, the BAIIPLUS™ calculator does have an Interest Conversion Worksheet that is discussed in the following example.

Example 22: Using the Interest Conversion Worksheet

For Example 21, compute the effective bi-weekly payment period rate and then use this rate to calculate the SUV bi-weekly loan payment.

Enter the SUV loan data below in the Interest Conversion Worksheet:

KEYSTROKES	DISPLAY
[2ND][FORMAT][8][ENTER]	DEC = 8.00000000
[CE/C]	8.00000000
[2ND][ICONV][3][ENTER]	NOM = 3.00000000
[↑][1][2][ENTER]	C/Y = 12.00000000
[↑][CPT]	EFF = 3.04159569
[↓][2][6][ENTER]	C/Y = 26.00000000
[↓][CPT]	NOM = 2.99798335

What we have accomplished so far is to convert the nominal annual interest rate based on monthly compounding to first an effective annual rate of 3.04159569% and then to convert this effective annual rate to a nominal annual interest rate of 2.99798335% based on bi-weekly compounding. Now that we have a nominal rate based on bi-weekly compounding, we can find the effective bi-weekly rate as 2.99798335%/26 = 0.11530705%.

To calculate the effective bi-weekly loan payment, press the [CE/C] to exit the Interest Conversion Worksheet.

Make sure that your calculator is set to the END mode and the BGN symbol is **not** displayed.

If BGN does appear, restore the calculator to the END mode by pressing the toggle switch keystroke sequence [2ND][BGN][2ND][SET][CE/C].

First, press [2ND][P/Y][1][ENTER] to set P/Y = 1.00000000.

Second, press [CE/C][2ND][CLR TVM] to clear the TVM memory registers.

Third, enter the following data:

KEYSTROKES	DISPLAY
[1][5][6][N]	N = 156.0000000
[.][1][1][5][3][0][7][0][5][I/Y]	I/Y = 0.11530705
[3][0][0][0][0][PV]	PV = 30,000.00000
[2ND][FORMAT][2][ENTER]	DEC = 2.00

Then press [CE/C][CPT][PMT] to obtain

PMT = -210.23.

This is precisely the payment that we previously calculated with much less effort.

Although the BAIIPLUS™ calculator does have an Interest Conversion Worksheet, it is really **not** necessary to use it unless there is a requirement to calculate the effective payment period rate. **On most other financial calculators, it is obligatory to make this conversion.**

Example 23: Canadian Mortgage with Monthly Payments

Suppose you want to buy a Canadian cottage on the shore of a quiet fishing lake in Northern Ontario. A Canadian bank quotes a nominal annual mortgage interest rate of 6% with semi-annual compounding for a 5-year term with amortization of 25 years. Your dream cottage costs $250,000 and you intend to pay $50,000 down. So, you want to borrow $200,000. Since you are paid a monthly salary, you want to make monthly mortgage payments. What is your monthly mortgage payment?

Unlike the U.S. customary monthly compounding of mortgage interest, Canadian banks must quote mortgage interest rates based on semi-annual compounding, **not** monthly compounding, in order to comply with the Bank Act of Canada. So, even when paying monthly, the payment frequency and the compounding frequency are different on all Canadian monthly mortgages.

Also note that the 5-year term of the mortgage is shorter than the 25-year amortization period. This means that the bank is only fixing the interest rate for 5 years, but payments will be calculated as if the bank were fixing the rate for 25 years. After 5 years, the interest rate and blended mortgage payment will be reset based on prevailing market rates.

Make sure that your calculator is set to the END mode and the BGN symbol is **not** displayed. If BGN does appear, restore the calculator to the END mode by pressing the toggle switch keystroke sequence [2ND][BGN][2ND][SET][CE/C].

First, press [2ND][P/Y][1][2][ENTER] to set P/Y = 12.00 and press [↓][2][ENTER] to set C/Y = 2.00.

Second, press [CE/C][2ND][CLR TVM].

Third, enter the following data:

KEYSTROKES	DISPLAY
[2][5][2ND][xP/Y][N]	300.00
[6][I/Y]	I/Y = 6.00
[2][0][0][0][0][0][PV]	PV = 200,000.00

Finally, press [CPT][PMT] to compute PMT = -1,279.61.

If you want to construct an amortization schedule for this mortgage, follow the **relevant steps in Example 18.**

CHAPTER 5

TVM CALCULATIONS: UNEVEN CASH FLOWS

Introduction

This chapter discusses how to calculate the present value (PV), future value (FV), internal rate of return (IRR), and net present value (NPV) of unequal cash flows.

Although one could use the TVM worksheet to do most of these calculations, it is generally quite cumbersome and time consuming to do so. Instead, the Cash Flow Worksheet is better suited to TVM calculations when cash flows are uneven, so its use will be described in this chapter.

Example 24: PV of Uneven Cash Flows

Assume the following cash flows (CFs):

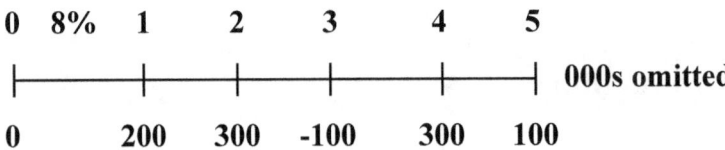

What is the present value (PV) of these cash flows (CFs) if the annual interest rate is 8%?

First, press the [CF] key to enter the Cash Flow Worksheet.

Second, press [2ND][CLR WORK] to clear any previous cash flow analyses.

Third, enter the cash flows:

KEYSTROKES	DISPLAY
[↓][2][0][0][0][0][0][ENTER]	C01 = 200,000.00
[↓][↓][3][0][0][0][0][0][ENTER]	C02 = 300,000.00
[↓][↓][1][0][0][0][0][0] [+/-][ENTER]	C03 = -100,000.00
[↓][↓][3][0][0][0][0][0][ENTER]	C04 = 300,000.00
[↓][↓][1][0][0][0][0][0][ENTER]	C05 = 100,000.00

Now the cash flows (CFs) have been entered.

Fourth, enter the interest rate by pressing [NPV][8][ENTER] and I = 8.00 will be displayed.

At this point, the BAIIPLUS™ knows the cash flows, the number of periods, and the interest rate.

Finally, press [↓][CPT] to compute the PV, which will be displayed as NPV = 651,570.88.

Note that the BAIIPLUS™ calls the cash flows C01, C02, etc. Why it does this will be clear with the next example.

Example 25: PV of Embedded Annuities

Assume the following cash flows, which contain embedded annuities of $200, $400, and $600:

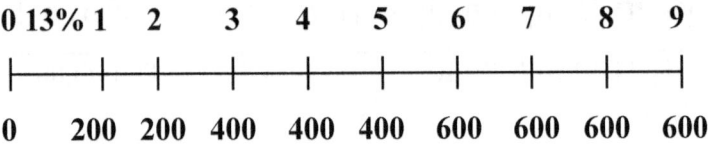

| 0 13% 1 | 2 | 3 | 4 | 5 | 6 | 7 | 8 | 9 |

| 0 | 200 | 200 | 400 | 400 | 400 | 600 | 600 | 600 | 600 |

What is the PV of these cash flows if the annual interest rate is 13%?

First, press the [CF] key to enter the Cash Flow Worksheet.

Second, press [2ND][CLR WORK] to clear any previous cash flow analyses.

Third, enter the cash flows:

KEYSTROKES	DISPLAY
[↓][2][0][0][ENTER]	C01 = 200.00
[↓][2][ENTER]	F01 = 2.00 (repeats C01 value 2x)
[↓][4][0][0][ENTER]	C02 = 400.00
[↓][3][ENTER]	F02 = 3.00 (repeats C02 value 3x)
[↓][6][0][0][ENTER]	C03 = 600.00
[↓][4][ENTER]	F03 = 4.00 (repeats C03 value 4x)

Now the BAIIPLUS™ knows the cash flows:

$CF_1 = CF_2 = C01 = 200.$

$CF_3 = CF_4 = CF_5 = C02 = 400.$

$CF_6 = CF_7 = CF_8 = CF_9 = C03 = 600.$

Thus, C01 represents the first embedded annuity, C02 represents the second embedded annuity, and C03 represents the third embedded annuity.

Fourth, press [NPV][1][3][ENTER] to enter the interest rate and I = 13.00 will be displayed.

At this point, the BAIIPLUS™ knows the cash flows, the number of periods, and the interest rate.

Finally, press [↓][CPT] to compute the PV, which is displayed as NPV = 2,041.93.

To check your entries, press the [CF] key. Then use the up and down arrow keys to view each cash flow.

Example 26: Internal Rate of Return (IRR) of an Investment

If you invest $10,000 today, you expect to receive the uneven set of cash flows shown in the timeline below:

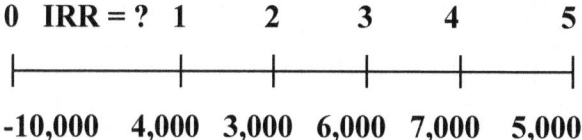

0 IRR = ?	1	2	3	4	5
-10,000	4,000	3,000	6,000	7,000	5,000

Should you make the investment if your required rate of return for investments of this degree of risk is 20%?

First, press the [CF] key to enter the Cash Flow Worksheet.

Second, press [2ND][CLR WORK] to clear any previous cash flow analyses.

Third, enter the cash flows:

KEYSTROKES	DISPLAY
[1][0][0][0][0][+/-][ENTER]	$CF_0 = -10,000.00$
[↓][4][0][0][0][ENTER]	$C01 = 4,000.00$
[↓][↓][3][0][0][0][ENTER]	$C02 = 3,000.00$
[↓][↓][6][0][0][0][ENTER]	$C03 = 6,000.00$
[↓][↓][7][0][0][0][ENTER]	$C04 = 7,000.00$
[↓][↓][5][0][0][0][ENTER]	$C05 = 5,000.00$

Now the BAIIPLUS™ knows the cash flows.

Finally, press [IRR][CPT] to compute the IRR = 36.35%.

Since the computed IRR exceeds your required rate of return of 20%, the investment should be accepted because it will increase your wealth.

Most people who calculate the IRR of an investment also calculate the net present value of that investment. See the next example.

Example 27: Net Present Value (NPV) of an Investment

Using the data from Example 26, you can also determine the NPV of this investment at your required rate of return of 20%.

If you still have the Example 26 data in your calculator, press [NPV][2][0][ENTER][↓][CPT] and the NPV of 4,274.05 will be displayed.

If you do not already have the data from Example 26 in your calculator, recall that the cash flows are shown in the timeline below:

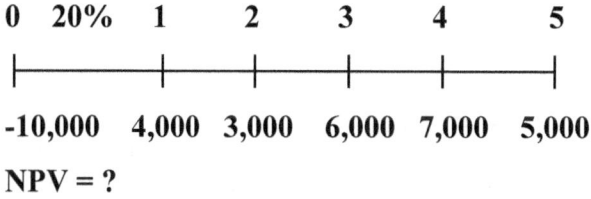

0   20%   1   2   3   4   5

-10,000   4,000   3,000   6,000   7,000   5,000

NPV = ?

First, press the [CF] key to enter the Cash Flow Worksheet.

Second, press [2ND][CLR WORK] to clear any previous cash flow analyses.

Third, enter the cash flows:

KEYSTROKES	DISPLAY
[1][0][0][0][0][+/-][ENTER]	CF_0 = -10,000.00
[↓][4][0][0][0][ENTER]	C01 = 4,000.00
[↓][↓][3][0][0][0][ENTER]	C02 = 3,000.00
[↓][↓][6][0][0][0][ENTER]	C03 = 6,000.00
[↓][↓][7][0][0][0][ENTER]	C04 = 7,000.00
[↓][↓][5][0][0][0][ENTER]	C05 = 5,000.00

Finally, press [NPV][2][0][ENTER][↓][CPT] and the NPV of 4,274.05 will be displayed. Thus, the PV of the cash inflows exceeds the cost of the investment by $4,274.05 at a discount rate of 20%. Therefore, this investment should be accepted because it will increase your wealth.

When an investment has normal cash flows (i.e. an outlay followed by a series of positive cash inflows) and is independent of any other investments, the decision to accept or reject the investment will be the same whether the IRR or NPV decision rule is used.

To be precise, NPV > 0 implies and is implied by IRR > required rate of return, leading to an increase in expected wealth by accepting the investment.

NPV < 0 implies and is implied by IRR < required rate of return. In this case, one should reject the investment because accepting the investment would lead to a decrease in expected wealth.

In theory, one should be indifferent if NPV = 0, which implies and is implied by the IRR = required rate of return.

In practice, the authors recommend rejection of the investment in this case because there is a tendency to be overly optimistic when estimating future cash inflows.

Example 28: Net Advantage to Leasing (NAL)

Suppose you wish to buy or lease a Tesla electric sports car. The dealer offers to sell you the car for $100,000. You can borrow $100,000 to finance the car over 48 months at a 6% nominal annual interest rate with monthly compounding. This implies that the effective monthly interest rate is 6%/12 = 0.5%.

Alternatively, the dealer will lease you the car. The 48 lease payments are $2,000 **each**, due at the **beginning** of each month with the last payment also due at the beginning of month 1 instead of month 48. Having 2 advance payments is typical of most automobile leases. If you wish to buy the car at the end of the 48-month lease, a residual value payment of $20,000 is required.

Should you buy the car now or lease it and then exercise the option to buy at the end of the lease?

To decide whether to buy or lease, you should calculate the net advantage to leasing (NAL). The NAL is the purchase price of the car **less** the present value of the lease payments including the residual value. The discount rate will be the 0.5% effective monthly interest rate for the car loan.

The timeline for the cash flows of the NAL analysis is:

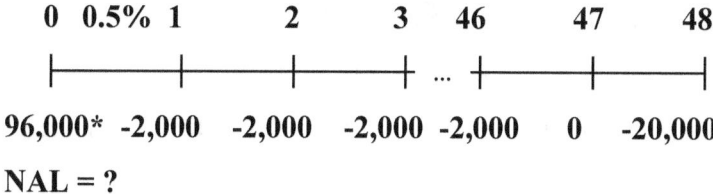

96,000* = \$100,000 purchase price - \$4,000 of lease payments due immediately

Note that the purchase price of the car always equals the PV of the blended monthly loan payments. For example, if the lender were charging a 9% nominal annual rate instead of 6%, the blended loan payments would be higher, but the PV of these higher loan payments based on the higher 9% rate would still be the purchase price of the car.

However, the PV of the fixed lease payments changes as the quoted loan rate changes. **The higher the loan rate, the lower is the PV of the lease payments.** Thus, leasing becomes more attractive as the loan rate rises.

Of course, as interest rates change in the economy as a whole, lease payments on new contracts can change. In this example, we focus on the fixed contract lease payments as we shop for loan rates among lenders.

First, press the [CF] key to enter the Cash Flow Worksheet.

Second, press [2ND][CLR WORK] to clear any previous cash flow analyses.

Third, enter the cash flows:

KEYSTROKES	DISPLAY
[9][6][0][0][0] [ENTER]	$CF_0 = 96,000.00$
[↓][2][0][0][0] [+/-][ENTER]	$C01 = -2,000.00$
[↓][46][ENTER]	$F01 = 46.00$ (repeats C01 value 46x)
[↓][0][ENTER]	$C02 = 0.00$
[↓][↓][2][0][0][0][0] [+/-][ENTER]	$C03 = -20,000.00$

Now the BAIIPLUS™ knows the cash flows.

The NAL is simply the NPV of the above cash flows calculated at the effective monthly interest rate of 0.5%.

Finally, press [NPV][.][5][ENTER][↓][CPT] to compute the NAL, which will be displayed as NPV = -1,746.34. Since the NAL is negative in this example, it is recommended that you buy the car for $100,000.

Example 29: NAL Breakeven Interest Rate

Using the data from Example 28, calculate the IRR that makes the NAL equal zero.

Recall that the timeline for the cash flows of the NAL analysis is:

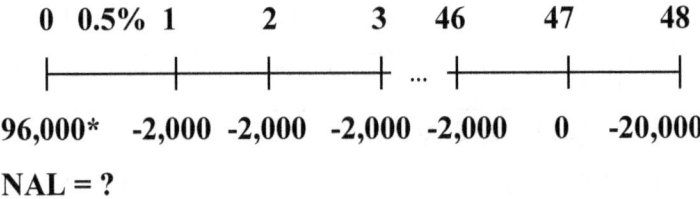

96,000* = \$100,000 purchase price - \$4,000 of lease payments due immediately

Before computing the IRR, change the number of decimal places to 8 by pressing [2ND][FORMAT][8][ENTER].

Then press [CE/C][IRR][CPT] and IRR = 0.56805925% per month is displayed.

The nominal annual breakeven interest rate based on monthly compounding is 12 x 0.56805925% = 6.81671105%.

The interpretation of this result is that for all nominal annual interest rates **above 6.81671105%, leasing will be more attractive because the NAL will be positive**. For all interest rates **below 6.81671105%, buying will be more attractive because the NAL will be negative**.

We have already shown that 6% < 6.81671105% gives a **negative** NAL in Example 28.

Let us obtain a positive NAL result by using 9% > 6.81671105%, which means that the effective monthly rate is 9%/12 = 0.75%.

Restore the number of decimal places to 2 by pressing [2ND][FORMAT][2][ENTER]. Then press [CE/C][NPV][.][7][5][ENTER] to display I = 0.75.

Finally, press [↓][CPT] to display NPV = 4,463.09. **Since the NAL is now positive, leasing is preferred.**

If the quoted nominal annual interest rate is 6.81671105% based on monthly compounding, then you should be indifferent between buying and leasing. Since the lease allows you to opt out of buying the car, this should be preferred because you could change your mind about owning this car in 4 years.

Let us conclude with 2 cautionary notes about leasing. Most leases have a mileage limit. If you exceed the allotted miles, then there can be rather high per mile charges for excess miles owing at the end of the lease if you opt **not** to buy the car then.

There also can be damage charges if you opt **not** to buy. So, if you elect to lease, make sure that you take good care of your car and watch your mileage limit. Otherwise, the option **not** to buy can be quite expensive to exercise.